Great Works

Instructional Guides for Literature

LITTLE BEAR

A guide for the book by Else Holmelund Minarik
Great Works Author: Tracy Pearce

SHELL EDUCATION

Publishing Credits

Owen Pearce, *Contributing Author*; Robin Erickson, *Production Director*;
Lee Aucoin, *Creative Director*; Timothy J. Bradley, *Illustration Manager*;
Emily R. Smith, M.A.Ed., *Editorial Director*; Amber Goff, *Editorial Assistant*;
Don Tran, *Production Supervisor*; Corinne Burton, M.A.Ed., *Publisher*

Image Credits

Cover and interior illustrations by Timothy J. Bradley and Stephanie Reid McGinley
Cover background image ylenkeat/Shutterstock

Standards

© 2007 Teachers of English to Speakers of Other Languages, Inc. (TESOL)
© 2007 Board of Regents of the University of Wisconsin System. World-Class Instructional Design and Assessment (WIDA)
© Copyright 2010. National Governors Association Center for Best Practices and Council of Chief State School Officers.
All rights reserved.

Shell Education

5301 Oceanus Drive
Huntington Beach, CA 92649-1030
http://www.shelleducation.com
ISBN 978-1-4258-8966-1
© 2014 Shell Educational Publishing, Inc.

Table of contents

How to Use This Literature Guide

Today's standards demand rigor and relevance in the reading of complex texts. The units in this series guide teachers in a rich and deep exploration of worthwhile works of literature for classroom study. The most rigorous instruction can also be interesting and engaging!

Many current strategies for effective literacy instruction have been incorporated into these instructional guides for literature. Throughout the units, text-dependent questions are used to determine comprehension of the book as well as student interpretation of the vocabulary words. The books chosen for the series are complex and are exemplars of carefully crafted works of literature. Close reading is used throughout the units to guide students toward revisiting the text and using textual evidence to respond to prompts orally and in writing. Students must analyze the story elements in multiple assignments for each section of the book. All of these strategies work together to rigorously guide students through their study of literature.

The next few pages will make clear how to use this guide for a purposeful and meaningful literature study. Each section of this guide is set up in the same way to make it easier for you to implement the instruction in your classroom.

Theme Thoughts

The great works of literature used throughout this series have important themes that have been relevant to people for many years. Many of the themes will be discussed during the various sections of this instructional guide. However, it would also benefit students to have independent time to think about the key themes of the book.

Before students begin reading, have them complete the *Pre-Reading Theme Thoughts* (page 13). This graphic organizer will allow students to think about the themes outside the context of the story. They'll have the opportunity to evaluate statements based on important themes and defend their opinions. Be sure to keep students' papers for comparison to the *Post-Reading Theme Thoughts* (page 58). This graphic organizer is similar to the pre-reading activity. However, this time, students will be answering the questions from the point of view of one of the characters in the book. They have to think about how the character would feel about each statement and defend their thoughts. To conclude the activity, have students compare what they thought about the themes before the book to what the characters discovered during the story.

How to Use This Literature Guide (cont.)

Vocabulary

Each teacher reference vocabulary overview page has definitions and sentences about how key vocabulary words are used in the section. These words should be introduced and discussed with students. Students will use these words in different activities throughout the book.

On some of the vocabulary student pages, students are asked to answer text-related questions about vocabulary words from the sections. The following question stems will help you create your own vocabulary questions if you'd like to extend the discussion.

- How does this word describe _____'s character?
- How does this word connect to the problem in this story?
- How does this word help you understand the setting?
- Tell me how this word connects to the main idea of this story.
- What visual pictures does this word bring to your mind?
- Why do you think the author used this word?

At times, you may find that more work with the words will help students understand their meanings and importance. These quick vocabulary activities are a good way to further study the words.

- Students can play vocabulary concentration. Make one set of cards that have the words on them and another set with the definitions. Then, have students lay them out on the table and play concentration. The goal of the game is to match vocabulary words with their definitions. For early readers or English language learners, the sets of cards could be the words and pictures of the words.

- Students can create word journal entries about the words. Students choose words they think are important and then describe why they think each word is important within the book. Early readers or English language learners could instead draw pictures about the words in a journal.

- Students can create puppets and use them to act out the vocabulary words from the stories. Artwork of the characters is provided on pages 59–61. Students can use these images to retell the stories using the vocabulary words. Students may also enjoy using the artwork to tell their own character-driven stories using vocabulary words from the original stories.

How to Use This Literature Guide (cont.)

Analyzing the Literature

After you have read each section with students, hold a small-group or whole-class discussion. Provided on the teacher reference page for each section are leveled questions. The questions are written at two levels of complexity to allow you to decide which questions best meet the needs of your students. The Level 1 questions are typically less abstract than the Level 2 questions. These questions are focused on the various story elements, such as character, setting, and plot. Be sure to add further questions as your students discuss what they've read. For each question, a few key points are provided for your reference as you discuss the book with students.

Reader Response

In today's classrooms, there are often great readers who are below average writers. So much time and energy is spent in classrooms getting students to read on grade level that little time is left to focus on writing skills. To help teachers include more writing in their daily literacy instruction, each section of this guide has a literature-based reader response prompt. Each of the three genres of writing is used in the reader responses within this guide: narrative, informative/explanatory, and opinion. Before students write, you may want to allow them time to draw pictures related to the topic. Book-themed writing paper is provided on page 70 if your students need more space to write.

Guided Close Reading

Within each section of this guide, it is suggested that you closely reread a portion of the text with your students. Page numbers are given, but since some versions of the books may have different page numbers, the sections to be reread are described by location as well. After rereading the section, there are a few text-dependent questions to be answered by students. A graphic organizer has been provided to help students prepare for the group discussion. They should record their thoughts and ideas on the graphic organizer and refer to it during your discussion. If your students are working above grade level, you may want to encourage them to respond to the questions in complete sentences.

Encourage students to read one question at a time and then go back to the text and discover the answer. Work with students to ensure that they use the text to determine their answers rather than making unsupported inferences. Suggested answers are provided in the answer key.

Introduction

How to Use This Literature Guide (cont.)

Guided Close Reading (cont.)

The generic open-ended stems below can be used to write your own text-dependent questions if you would like to give students more practice.

- What words in the story support . . . ?
- What text helps you understand . . . ?
- Use the book to tell why _____ happens.
- Based on the events in the story, . . . ?
- Show me the part in the text that supports . . . .
- Use the text to tell why . . . .

Making Connections

The activities in this section help students make cross-curricular connections to mathematics, science, social studies, fine arts, or other curricular areas. These activities require higher-order thinking skills from students but also allow for creative thinking.

Language Learning

A special section has been set aside to connect the literature to language conventions. Through these activities, students will have opportunities to practice the conventions of standard English grammar, usage, capitalization, and punctuation.

Story Elements

It is important to spend time discussing what the common story elements are in literature. Understanding the characters, setting, plot, and theme can increase students' comprehension and appreciation of the story. If teachers begin discussing those elements in early childhood, students will more likely internalize the concepts and look for the elements in their independent reading. Another very important reason for focusing on the story elements is that students will be better writers if they think about how the stories they read are constructed.

In the story elements activities, students are asked to create work related to the characters, setting, or plot. Consider having students complete only one of these activities. If you give students a choice on this assignment, each student can decide to complete the activity that most appeals to him or her. Different intelligences are used so that the activities are diverse and interesting to all students.

How to Use This Literature Guide (cont.)

Culminating Activity

At the end of this instructional guide is a creative culminating activity that allows students the opportunity to share what they've learned from reading the book. This activity is open ended so that students can push themselves to create their own great works within your language arts classroom.

Comprehension Assessment

The questions in this section require students to think about the book they've read as well as the words that were used in the book. Some questions are tied to quotations from the book to engage students and require them to think about the text as they answer the questions.

Response to Literature

Finally, students are asked to respond to the literature by drawing pictures and writing about the characters and stories. A suggested rubric is provided for teacher reference.

Correlation to the Standards

Shell Education is committed to producing educational materials that are research and standards based. In this effort, we have correlated all of our products to the academic standards of all 50 United States, the District of Columbia, the Department of Defense Dependents Schools, and all Canadian provinces.

Purpose and Intent of Standards

Standards are designed to focus instruction and guide adoption of curricula. Standards are statements that describe the criteria necessary for students to meet specific academic goals. They define the knowledge, skills, and content students should acquire at each level. Standards are also used to develop standardized tests to evaluate students' academic progress. Teachers are required to demonstrate how their lessons meet standards. Standards are used in the development of all of our products, so educators can be assured they meet high academic standards.

How To Find Standards Correlations

To print a customized correlation report of this product for your state, visit our website at http://www.shelleducation.com and follow the online directions. If you require assistance in printing correlation reports, please contact Customer Service at 1-877-777-3450.

correlation to the Standards (cont.)

Standards correlation chart

The lessons in this guide were written to support the Common Core College and Career Readiness Anchor Standards. This chart indicates which sections of this guide address the anchor standards.

Common Core College and Career Readiness Anchor Standard	Section
CCSS.ELA-Literacy.CCRA.R.1—Read closely to determine what the text says explicitly and to make logical inferences from it; cite specific textual evidence when writing or speaking to support conclusions drawn from the text.	Guided Close Reading Sections 1–5; Story Elements Sections 1–4
CCSS.ELA-Literacy.CCRA.R.2—Determine central ideas or themes of a text and analyze their development; summarize the key supporting details and ideas.	Analyzing the Literature Sections 1–5; Guided Close Reading Sections 1–5; Post-Reading Response to Literature
CCSS.ELA-Literacy.CCRA.R.3—Analyze how and why individuals, events, or ideas develop and interact over the course of a text.	Analyzing the Literature Sections 1–5; Guided Close Reading Sections 1–5; Story Elements Section 2; Post-Reading Response to Literature
CCSS.ELA-Literacy.CCRA.R.4—Interpret words and phrases as they are used in a text, including determining technical, connotative, and figurative meanings, and analyze how specific word choices shape meaning or tone.	Vocabulary Sections 1–5; Guided Close Reading Sections 1–5
CCSS.ELA-Literacy.CCRA.R.5—Analyze the structure of texts, including how specific sentences, paragraphs, and larger portions of the text (e.g., a section, a chapter) relate to each other and the whole.	Analyzing the Literature Sections 1–5
CCSS.ELA-Literacy.CCRA.R.9—Analyze how two or more texts address similar themes or topics in order to build knowledge or to compare the approaches the authors take.	Making Connections Section 2
CCSS.ELA-Literacy.CCRA.R.10—Read and comprehend complex literary and informational texts independently and proficiently.	Entire Unit
CCSS.ELA-Literacy.CCRA.W.1—Write arguments to support claims in an analysis of substantive topics or texts using valid reasoning and relevant and sufficient evidence.	Reader Response Section 2; Making Connections Section 1
CCSS.ELA-Literacy.CCRA.W.2—Write informative/explanatory texts to examine and convey complex ideas and information clearly and accurately through the effective selection, organization, and analysis of content.	Reader Response Sections 3, 5; Post-Reading Response to Literature

correlation to the standards (cont.)

standards correlation chart (cont.)

Common Core College and Career Readiness Anchor Standard	Section
CCSS.ELA-Literacy.CCRA.W.3—Write narratives to develop real or imagined experiences or events using effective technique, well-chosen details, and well-structured event sequences.	Reader Response Sections 1, 4; Story Elements Sections 1–4; Making Connections Section 4
CCSS.ELA-Literacy.CCRA.W.4—Produce clear and coherent writing in which the development, organization, and style are appropriate to task, purpose, and audience.	Story Elements Sections 3–4; Making Connections Section 4; Culminating Activity
CCSS.ELA-Literacy.CCRA.L.1—Demonstrate command of the conventions of standard English grammar and usage when writing or speaking.	Analyzing the Literature Sections 1–5; Guided Close Reading Sections 1–5; Language Learning Sections 1, 3
CCSS.ELA-Literacy.CCRA.L.2—Demonstrate command of the conventions of standard English capitalization, punctuation, and spelling when writing.	Analyzing the Literature Sections 1–5; Guided Close Reading Sections 1–5; Language Learning Sections 2, 4
CCSS.ELA-Literacy.CCRA.L.4—Determine or clarify the meaning of unknown and multiple-meaning words and phrases by using context clues, analyzing meaningful word parts, and consulting general and specialized reference materials, as appropriate.	Vocabulary Sections 1–5
CCSS.ELA-Literacy.CCRA.L.6—Acquire and use accurately a range of general academic and domain-specific words and phrases sufficient for reading, writing, speaking, and listening at the colleges and career readiness level; demonstrate independence in gathering vocabulary knowledge when encountering an unknown term important to comprehension or expression.	Vocabulary Sections 1–5

TESOL and WIDA Standards

The lessons in this book promote English language development for English language learners. The following TESOL and WIDA English Language Development Standards are addressed through the activities in this book:

- **Standard 1:** English language learners communicate for social and instructional purposes within the school setting.

- **Standard 2:** English language learners communicate information, ideas and concepts necessary for academic success in the content area of language arts.

About the Author—Else Holmelund Minarik

Else Holmelund Minarik was born on September 13, 1920, in Denmark. While she lived in Denmark, she started her love of reading with the stories from her favorite writer, Hans Christian Andersen. At the young age of four, she moved with her family to New York.

Minarik studied psychology and art at Queens College and became a reporter for the Daily Sentinel in Rome, New York. During World War II, she responded to the lack of teachers by becoming a first grade teacher in Long Island, New York.

While Minarik was teaching first graders and raising her daughter, she realized that there was a need for books that both engaged readers and were easy to read through sounding out syllables. The first Little Bear book was written and mimeographed for her students to read. The book was very popular with her students so she decided to take it to Harper and Bros. In 1995, fans of the Little Bear stories were able to follow the adventures of Little Bear in an animated television series.

Minarik, who died in 1991, will always be remembered for her first book, *Little Bear*, which was the inaugural title in the I Can Read! series. During her five-decade career, she wrote more than 40 children's books and helped generations of youngsters learn to read.

Possible Texts for Text Comparisons

There are four other books in this Else Holmelund Minarik series: *Father Bear Comes Home*, *Little Bear's Friend*, *Little Bear's Visit*, and *A Kiss for Little Bear*. *Cats and Dogs* and *No Fighting, No Biting!* may also be used for enriching text comparisons by the same author.

Cross-curricular connection

This book could be used in a science unit on the study of bears or the moon. This book could also be used in a social studies unit on birthdays.

Book Summary of *Little Bear*

The main characters, Little Bear and Mother Bear, have a delightful, loving relationship. Mother Bear uses a gentle, teasing approach with Little Bear. Little Bear has a way of winning Mother Bear's approval and encouragement. Little Bear is a lovable son and a fine friend to Duck, Hen, and Cat. Little Bear goes on many adventures in a variety of charming stories in five books. The stories are filled with warmth, imagination, and humor as Little Bear explores life.

In *Little Bear*, four different stories introduce readers to Little Bear's adventures.

- In "What Will Little Bear Wear?" Little Bear is first introduced. Little Bear wants to play outside but worries it will be too cold. Little Bear adds pieces of clothing and becomes all bundled up, but he is still cold. Soon he realizes, with the help of Mother Bear, that he needs a fur coat, which, luckily, he has.

- In "Birthday Soup," Little Bear cannot find his mother and he thinks she forgot his birthday. So he decides to make birthday soup for his friends only to find out that his mother has remembered his birthday.

- In "Little Bear Goes to the Moon," Little Bear goes on a pretend trip to the moon wearing his new space helmet. Mother Bear lets him go as long as he is back by lunch.

- In "Little Bear's Wish," Little Bear has many wishes just before bedtime, but Mother Bear knows he cannot have all his wishes. So, Mother Bear tells Little Bear a bedtime story about his exciting day.

Possible Texts for Text Sets

- Freeman, Don. *Corduroy*. Puffin, 1976.
- Hodge, Deborah. *Bears: Polar Bears, Black Bears, and Grizzly Bears*. Kids Can Press, 1996.
- Wilson, Karma. *Bear Snores On*. Little Simon, 2005.

or

- Brown, Margaret Wise. *Goodnight Moon*. HarperFestival, 2007.
- Carle, Eric. *Papa, Please Get the Moon for Me*. Little Simon, 1999.
- Gibbons, Gail. *The Moon Book*. Holiday House, 1998.

or

- Asch, Frank. *Happy Birthday, Moon*. Aladdin, 2000.
- Hoban, Russell. *A Birthday for Frances*. HarperCollins, 1976.
- Seuss, Dr. *Happy Birthday to You!*. Random House Books for Young Readers, 1959.

Pre-Reading Theme Thoughts

Directions: Draw a picture of a happy face or a sad face. Your face should show how you feel about each statement. Then, use words to say what you think about each statement.

Statement	How Do You Feel? 😊 ☹️	Explain Your Answer
You look and look. But, you already have what you need.		
Somebody forgot your birthday.		
You can go anywhere in your imagination.		
Time for bed!		

Vocabulary Overview

Key words and phrases from this section are provided below with definitions and sentences about how the words are used in the story. Introduce and discuss these important vocabulary words with students. If you think these words or other words in the story warrant more time devoted to them, there are suggestions in the introduction for other vocabulary activities (page 5).

Word	Definition	Sentence About Text
cold (p. 11)	having a very low temperature	It is snowing, and Little Bear is **cold**.
snow (p. 11)	soft, white pieces of frozen water that fall to the ground from the sky in cold weather	It is cold, and the **snow** falls from the sky.
come down (p. 11)	falls to the ground, especially in large amounts	Mother Bear sees the snow **come down**.
something (p. 11)	a thing that is not known, named, or specified	Little Bear wants **something** to keep warm.
hurray (p. 13)	used to express joy, approval, or encouragement	Little Bear says, "**Hurray**!" when he is not cold.
put on (p. 14)	to dress yourself in clothing	Little Bear **puts on** a hat.
coat (p. 15)	an outer piece of clothing that is worn to keep warm or dry	Mother Bear gives Little Bear a **coat** to wear.
again (p. 16)	for another time	Little Bear comes back to Mother Bear **again**.
snow pants (p. 17)	pants made of waterproof fabric that are worn during play activities in the snow	Little Bear is happy to wear **snow pants**.
fur (p. 20)	the hairy coat of an animal especially when it is soft and thick	Little Bear is covered with **fur**.

Name _____

Vocabulary Activity

Directions: Choose at least two words from the story. Draw a picture that shows what these words mean. Label your picture.

Words from the Story

cold	snow	come down	something	hurray
put on	coat	again	snow pants	fur

Directions: Answer this question.

1. Why does Little Bear think he is **cold**?

_____

_ _

_____

Analyzing the Literature

Provided below are discussion questions you can use in small groups, with the whole class, or for written assignments. Each question is written at two levels so you can choose the right question for each group of students. For each question, a few key points are provided for your reference as you discuss the book with students.

Story Element	Level 1	Level 2	Key Discussion Points
Plot	What is the problem in the story?	Describe the problem in the story.	The problem is that Little Bear feels that it is cold because the snow is coming down. Little Bear tries to put on various items of clothing to be warm, but he realizes he already has a fur coat.
Character	How do you know that Mother Bear is helping Little Bear?	In what ways does Mother Bear help Little Bear in the story?	Mother Bear stops what she is doing every time Little Bear comes in and says he is cold. Mother Bear gives him something new each time. She is very helpful and patient with him.
Plot	What does Mother Bear say at the end of the story?	What is funny about the ending of this story?	Mother Bear says, "What do you think of that?" at the end of the story. It is funny because he was born with a fur coat and had it all along.
Setting	What is the setting of the story?	Describe the setting of the story.	The story takes place inside and outside Little Bear's home. Students should use the pictures to gather information about the setting.

Name _____

Reader Response

Think

In this story, Little Bear just can't get warm! Think about a time when you were caught in bad weather.

Narrative Writing Prompt

Write about a time when you were very cold or very hot. What did you do to feel better?

_____

_____

_____

_____

_____

_____

_____

_____

_____

_____

_____

_____

Name _____

Guided close Reading

Closely reread when Mother Bear gives Little Bear his coat (pages 14–15).

Directions: Think about these questions. In the chart, write ideas or draw pictures as you think. Be ready to share your answers.

❶ Look at the pictures closely to see what chore Mother Bear is doing when Little Bear tells her that he is cold and wants something.

❷ Describe what Mother Bear gives Little Bear.

❸ What text tells you that Little Bear is happy with what Mother Bear gives him?

Name _____

Making Connections—Real or Acting Like People?

Directions: Many stories have characters that are animals. These animals do things that real animals cannot do. Fill in the Venn diagram below to show what you know about real bears and bears that act like people.

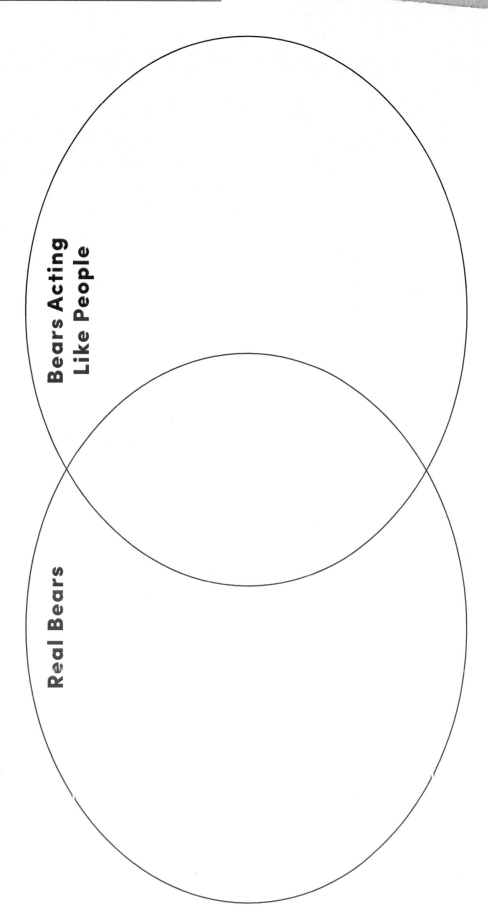

Bears Acting Like People

Real Bears

Name _____

Making connections—creating a Play

Directions: Make paper dolls for Mother Bear and Little Bear. Color Mother Bear and Little Bear. Color the clothes for Little Bear on the next page. Act out the story with the paper dolls and the clothing.

Making connections—creating a Play *(cont.)*

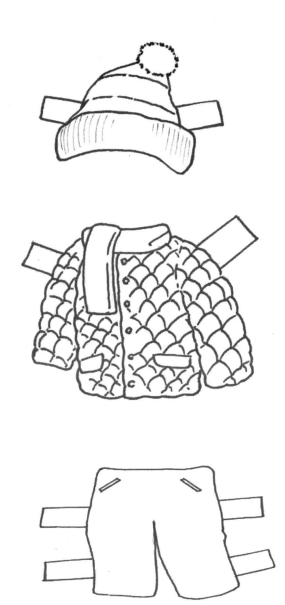

Name _____

Language Learning—Exclamations!

Directions: Write at least three sentences about cold weather. Each one must end with an exclamation point.

_____

- - - - - - - - - - - - - - - - - - -

_____

- - - - - - - - - - - - - - - - - - -

_____

- - - - - - - - - - - - - - - - - - -

_____

- - - - - - - - - - - - - - - - - - -

_____

- - - - - - - - - - - - - - - - - - -

_____

- - - - - - - - - - - - - - - - - - -

_____

- - - - - - - - - - - - - - - - - - -

_____

- - - - - - - - - - - - - - - - - - -

_____

Name _____

Story Elements—Setting

Directions: Draw a picture of Mother Bear and Little Bear. Show them outside their home in the winter.

Name _____

Story Elements—Plot

Directions: The events in a story are part of the plot. Fill in the missing events from this story.

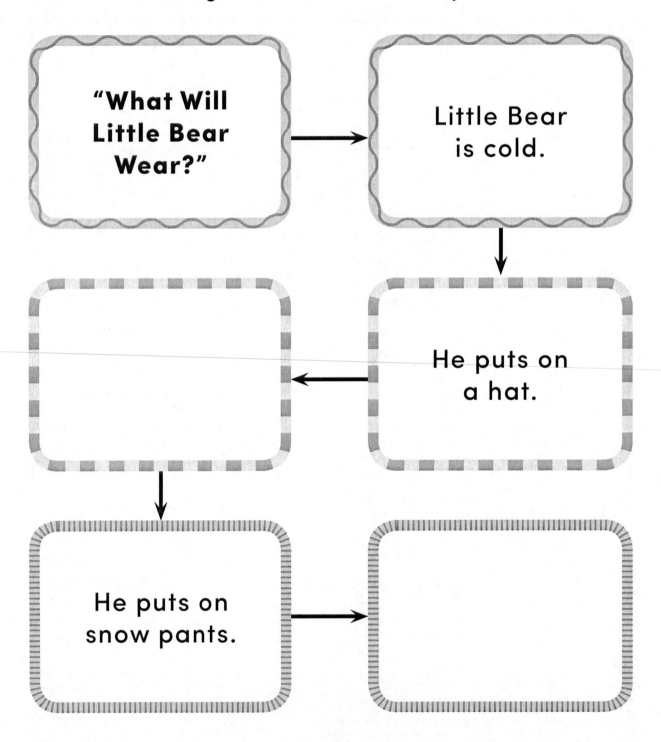

"What Will Little Bear Wear?"

Little Bear is cold.

He puts on a hat.

He puts on snow pants.

Vocabulary Overview

Key words and phrases from this section are provided below with definitions and sentences about how the words are used in the story. Introduce and discuss these important vocabulary words with students. If you think these words or other words in the story warrant more time devoted to them, there are suggestions in the introduction for other vocabulary activities (page 5).

Word	Definition	Sentence About Text
birthday (p. 22)	the day when someone was born or the anniversary of that day	Today is Little Bear's **birthday**.
soup (p. 23)	a food made by cooking vegetables, meat, or fish in a large amount of liquid	The **soup** has carrots, potatoes, peas, and tomatoes.
smells (p. 25)	the quality of a thing that you can sense with your nose	The soup **smells** very good.
wait (p. 25)	to stay in a place until an expected event happens	His friends will **wait** for the soup.
cook (p. 29)	to prepare food for eating, especially by using heat	Little Bear will **cook** some hot soup.
shut (p. 32)	to close	Little Bear is told to **shut** his eyes.
beautiful (p. 34)	giving pleasure to the mind or the senses	The cake Mother Bear makes is **beautiful**.
forget (p. 34)	to be unable to think of or remember something	Little Bear is happy that Mother Bear did not **forget** his birthday.
surprise (p. 34)	an unexpected gift or party	Mother Bear has a **surprise** for Little Bear.
never (p. 34)	not ever; not at any time	Mother Bear will **never** forget Little Bear's birthday.

Name _____

Vocabulary Activity

Directions: Draw lines to complete the sentences.

Beginnings of Sentences	Ends of Sentences
Little Bear can't **wait**	coming over for his **birthday**.
Something **smells** good	**surprise** for Little Bear.
Little Bear makes his	**soup** in a black pot.
Little Bear's friends are	to turn a year older.
Mother Bear bakes a	in Little Bear's house.

Directions: Answer this question.

1. Why will Mother Bear **never forget** Little Bear's birthday?

_____

_____

_____

Analyzing the Literature

Provided below are discussion questions you can use in small groups, with the whole class, or for written assignments. Each question is written at two levels so you can choose the right question for each group of students. For each question, a few key points are provided for your reference as you discuss the book with students.

Story Element	Level 1	Level 2	Key Discussion Points
Character	Why does Little Bear make birthday soup?	Why is it important for Little Bear to make birthday soup?	Little Bear thinks Mother Bear is not home. He does not see a birthday cake, and his friends are coming over. His friends like soup, so he makes soup for his birthday.
Plot	What gifts do Little Bear's friends bring to him?	How do the illustrations or pictures help you to find out what each friend brings to Little Bear?	Hen, Duck, and Cat each bring a different gift to Little Bear. The pictures help to add details to the text of the story.
Setting	What is the setting of this story?	The setting of a story is not only what we can see but also what we can smell and hear. Describe the setting of this story.	This story takes place in Little Bear's home. It shows the cooking area, the dining table, and the door that is hiding Mother Bear. The smell of the yummy soup is in the air.
Character	What lesson does Little Bear learn?	How does Little Bear learn the lesson in this story?	Little Bear learns that Mother Bear does not forget his birthday and never will. He learns that Mother Bear knows it is his birthday all along. She has a birthday cake for him.

Name _____

Reader Response

Think

Think about your favorite birthday gifts. What types of gifts do you like to receive?

Opinion Writing Prompt

Describe the best birthday gift you ever got. Explain why it was so amazing.

_____

_____

_____

_____

_____

_____

_____

_____

_____

_____

_____

_____

Name _____

Guided close Reading

Closely reread the first two pages of the story (pages 22–23), where Little Bear cannot find Mother Bear.

Directions: Think about these questions. In the chart, write ideas or draw pictures as you think. Be ready to share your answers.

❶ Based on the events in the story, why does Little Bear think that Mother Bear has not made a birthday cake for him?

❷ Use the book to tell why Little Bear decides to make birthday soup.

❸ What ingredients does Little Bear put into the soup?

Name _____

Making connections—Different and Alike

Directions: Read *Happy Birthday, Moon* by Frank Asch. Fill in the Venn diagram below.

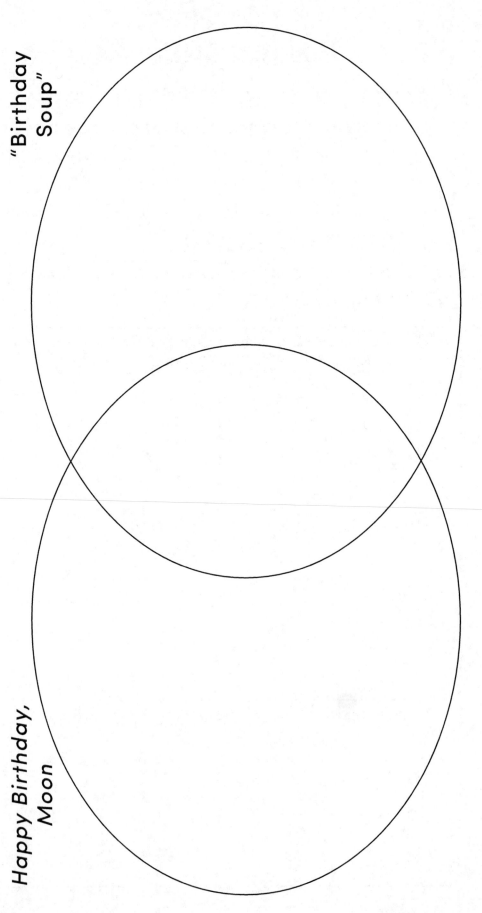

"Birthday Soup"

Happy Birthday, Moon

 #40003—Instructional Guide: Little Bear

Name _____

Making connections—Poetry

Directions: Think about a birthday party that you have been to. Write a poem about that party.

_____

- - - - - - - - - - - - - - - - - - - -

_____

- - - - - - - - - - - - - - - - - - - -

_____

_____

- - - - - - - - - - - - - - - - - - - -

_____

_____

- - - - - - - - - - - - - - - - - - - -

_____

- - - - - - - - - - - - - - - - - - - -

_____

Name _____

Language Learning—Capital Letters

Directions: Make a list of five main events in the story. Each event must have at least one word that starts with a capital letter. An example has been done for you.

Example: Little Bear calls Mother.

- _____
  _____

- _____
  _____

- _____
  _____

- _____
  _____

- _____
  _____

Name _____

Story Elements—Setting

Directions: Draw a picture of the setting of this story. Be sure to include the soup Little Bear makes. Also show the beautiful birthday cake Mother Bear makes.

Name _____

Story Elements—Plot

Directions: Little Bear put carrots, potatoes, peas, and tomatoes in his birthday soup. What foods would you like to put in your birthday soup? Draw your ingredients in the pot. Make a list of the ingredients on the pot.

Name _____

Story Elements—character

Directions: Draw a picture of a friend who came to Little Bear's home. Write the name of the friend. Then, draw a picture of what the friend brought to Little Bear.

Friend

_____

— — — — — — — — — — — — — —

_____

Gift

Vocabulary Overview

Key words and phrases from this section are provided below with definitions and sentences about how the words are used in the story. Introduce and discuss these important vocabulary words with students. If you think these words or other words in the story warrant more time devoted to them, there are suggestions in the introduction for other vocabulary activities (page 5).

Word	Definition	Sentence About Text
space (p. 36)	the area around Earth where there are stars and planets	Little Bear puts on a **space** helmet.
helmet (p. 36)	a hard hat that is worn to protect your head	Little Bear makes a **helmet** to go to the moon.
moon (p. 36)	the large round object that circles Earth and that shines at night by reflecting light from the sun	Little Bear wants to fly to the **moon**.
wings (p. 38)	a part of an animal's body that is used for flying or gliding	Birds have **wings**, but Little Bear has no wings.
feathers (p. 38)	the light, flat growths that are the outer covering of the body of a bird	Birds have both wings and **feathers**.
plop (p. 38)	to allow your body to drop heavily or carelessly	When Little Bear jumps, he comes down with a big **plop**.
climbed (p. 41)	to move or go up/down something using your feet and often your hands	Little Bear **climbs** the tree.
tumbled (p. 42)	to fall down suddenly and quickly	He **tumbles** down the hill.
earth (p. 43)	the planet on which we live	Little Bear thinks the moon looks like **Earth**.
fooling (p. 48)	to make someone believe something that is not true; to trick	Mother Bear is **fooling** Little Bear.

Name _____

Vocabulary Activity

Directions: Write at least two sentences using words from the story.

Words from the Story

space	helmet	moon	wings	feathers
plop	climbed	tumbled	earth	fooling

_____

- -

_____

_____

- -

_____

_____

- -

_____

_____

- -

_____

Directions: Answer this question.
1. Why does Mother Bear say Little Bear has no **wings**?

_____

- -

_____

_____

- -

_____

Analyzing the Literature

Provided below are discussion questions you can use in small groups, with the whole class, or for written assignments. Each question is written at two levels so you can choose the right question for each group of students. For each question, a few key points are provided for your reference as you discuss the book with students.

Story Element	Level 1	Level 2	Key Discussion Points
Character	What is the last thing that Mother Bear tells Little Bear to do before he leaves for the moon?	Describe what Mother Bear says to Little Bear before he leaves for the moon. Why do you think Mother Bear says that?	Mother Bear lets Little Bear go to the moon as long as he is back in time for lunch. She allows him to go have fun and explore.
Setting	What does the moon look like in this story?	Why does the moon look like Earth in this story?	Little Bear thinks the moon looks just like Earth. The trees and birds look the same. There is even a house that looks just like his.
Plot	How does Little Bear get to the moon?	Describe how Little Bear gets to the moon.	Little Bear looks for a good high spot. He finds a tree on top of a hill and closes his eyes to jump. When he lands he thinks he is on the moon.
Character	Why does Mother Bear pretend that Little Bear is someone else?	Explain how Mother Bear pretends that Little Bear is someone else.	Mother Bear pretends that Little Bear is a bear from Earth and they are both on the moon. Perhaps she does this so Little Bear can continue with this imagination game.

Reader Response

Think

Think about the moon. What facts do you know?
How does the moon look?

Informative/Explanatory Writing Prompt

Describe the moon for someone who has never seen it.

_____

- -

_____

- -

_____

- -

_____

- -

_____

- -

_____

- -

_____

- -

_____

Name _____

Guided Close Reading

Closely reread from where Mother Bear pretends that Little Bear is a bear from Earth to the end of the story (pages 46–48).

Directions: Think about these questions. In the chart, write ideas or draw pictures as you think. Be ready to share your answers.

---

❶ What words or sentences in the story show you that Mother Bear is pretending to be on the moon?

---

❷ How does the author show us that Little Bear understands that Mother Bear is pretending for him?

---

❸ What connections can you make between your family and how Mother Bear plays make-believe with Little Bear?

Name _____

Making connections—
Phases of the Moon

Directions: Little Bear wants to go to the moon. Help him understand the different phases of the moon. Match the moons with their names. Draw a line to match each one.

   **new moon**

   **full moon**

   **half moon**

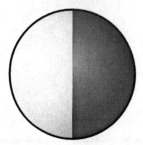   **crescent moon**

Name _____

Making connections—comic strip

Directions: Make a comic strip of this Little Bear story. Use speech bubbles to show what Little Bear and Mother Bear are saying.

Name _____

Language Learning—Adjectives

Directions: Think about Little Bear and Mother Bear.
What do you know about them? Write at least three
adjectives to tell about each character. Examples
have been given for you.

Little Bear	Mother Bear
friendly	loving

Name _____

Story Elements—Plot

Directions: Fill in what happened next.

Little Bear has a new space helmet.

_____
- - - - - - - - - - - - - -
_____
- - - - - - - - - - - - - -
_____
- - - - - - - - - - - - - -
_____

Little Bear finds a house that looks just like his house.

_____
- - - - - - - - - - - - - -
_____
- - - - - - - - - - - - - -
_____
- - - - - - - - - - - - - -
_____

#40003—Instructional Guide: Little Bear

Story Elements—Character

Directions: Draw a picture of Little Bear tying to get to the moon. You can include him trying to fly, climb, and tumble. Use descriptive words to write at least two labels for your picture.

Name _____

Story Elements—Setting

Directions: Create a three-dimensional image that shows Little Bear on the moon. Think of clever ways to create the birds and trees so that they are not flat. Little Bear should be in your picture. Can you make him stand up off your paper?

Vocabulary Overview

Key words and phrases from this section are provided below with definitions and sentences about how the words are used in the story. Introduce and discuss these important vocabulary words with students. If you think these words or other words in the story warrant more time devoted to them, there are suggestions in the introduction for other vocabulary activities (page 5).

Word	Definition	Sentence About Text
asleep (p. 51)	in a state of sleep; sleeping	Mother Bear wants Little Bear to be **asleep**.
wishing (p. 51)	to want something to be true or to happen	Little Bear is **wishing** for a story.
cloud (p. 52)	a white or gray mass in the sky that is made of many very small drops of water	Little Bear wants to sit on a **cloud** and fly around.
Viking boat (p. 53)	a narrow open vessel with oars and a sail used by Vikings during medieval times	A **Viking boat** sails on the ocean.
tunnel (p. 54)	a passage that goes under the ground or through a hill	Little Bear wants to go through a **tunnel**.
China (p. 54)	a country in Asia	He wants to go all the way to **China**.
chopsticks (p. 54)	thin sticks that are used especially by people in Asia to pick up and eat food	Little Bear could get **chopsticks** for Mother Bear.
castle (p. 55)	a large building with high, thick walls and towers that was built in the past to protect against attack	Little Bear could come to a big **castle**.
princess (p. 56)	a female member of a royal family	A **princess** could give Little Bear some cake.
good night (p. 60)	used to express good wishes in the evening, especially when someone is leaving or going to sleep	Mother Bear tells Little Bear **good night** before he goes to sleep.

Name _____

Vocabulary Activity

Directions: Complete each sentence below with one of the vocabulary words listed here.

Words from the Story

asleep	wishing	cloud	Viking boat	tunnel
China	chopsticks	castle	princess	good night

1. Mother Bear asks Little Bear why he is not
_____.

2. Little Bear is _____ for many things.

3. Little Bear wishes he could sit on a _____
and fly around.

4. A _____ might bring some cake.

Directions: Answer this question.

5. Where does Little Bear want to go to get **chopsticks**
for Mother Bear?

_____

_ _

_____

Analyzing the Literature

Provided below are discussion questions you can use in small groups, with the whole class, or for written assignments. Each question is written at two levels so you can choose the right question for each group of students. For each question, a few key points are provided for your reference as you discuss the book with students.

Story Element	Level 1	Level 2	Key Discussion Points
Setting	Describe one of the settings in this story.	Describe some of the settings in this story.	Little Bear wishes for many adventures. These adventures take him to many different settings: a cloud, the ocean looking at a Viking boat, a tunnel going to China, a big castle eating cake with a princess, and his own bed.
Plot	What is the problem in this story?	Describe the problem in this story and how it is solved.	Little Bear is not asleep because he is wishing. Mother Bear tells Little Bear that many of his wishes cannot come true. His wish to hear a story about things he once did can be granted. Finally, Little Bear goes to sleep after Mother Bear tells him a story.
Plot	What type of story did Little Bear want to hear from Mother Bear?	Describe the stories that Mother Bear tells Little Bear.	Mother Bear tells Little Bear stories about things he once did. She tells him about playing in the snow, wanting to fly to the moon, and making birthday soup.
Character	At the end of this story, how can Little Bear make Mother Bear happy?	Describe how Little Bear makes Mother Bear happy at the end of this story.	Little Bear makes Mother Bear happy by going to sleep for the night.

Name _____

Reader Response

Think

Think about your favorite bedtime story. Who tells the story to you? What is the story about?

Narrative Writing Prompt

Retell your favorite bedtime story with lots of details.

_____

_____

_____

_____

_____

_____

_____

_____

_____

_____

_____

_____

Name _____

Guided Close Reading

Closely reread page 57 where Little Bear says he would like to hear a story.

Directions: Think about these questions. In the chart, write ideas or draw pictures as you think. Be ready to share your answers.

❶ What text helps you understand what Little Bear wants from Mother Bear?

❷ Based on the text, what kind of story does Little Bear want to hear?

❸ Look closely at the pictures and describe where Little Bear and Mother Bear are in this part of the story.

Name _____

Making connections— What Do You Wish For?

Directions: Draw a picture of something that you wish for. Write at least two sentences about your wish.

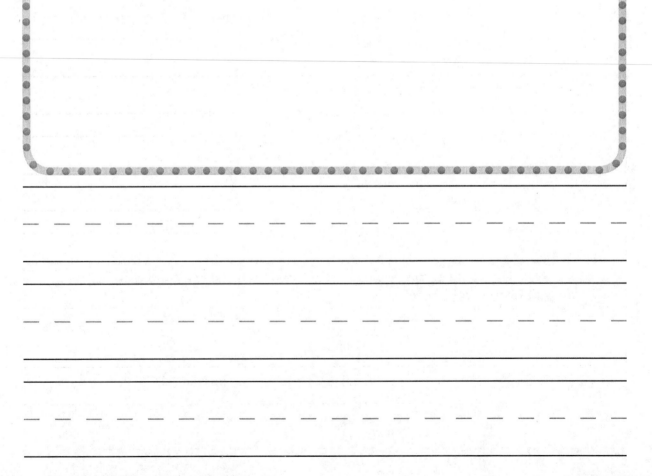

_____

- -

_____

- -

_____

- -

_____

 #40003—Instructional Guide: Little Bear

Name _____

Making connections—Songs

Directions: Write a song about how Mother Bear and Little Bear treat each other. Use all the stories that you have read to get ideas.

_____

- -

_____

- -

_____

- -

_____

- -

_____

- -

_____

- -

_____

- -

_____

- -

_____

- -

_____

Name _____

Language Learning—Dialogue

Directions: Write a new scene. Include another wish that Little Bear might have.

_____

" _ _ _ _ _ _ _ _ _ _ _ _ _ _ _ _ _ _ _

_____

_ _ _ _ _ _ _ _ _ _ _ _ _ _ _ _ _ "

_____

_ _ _ _ _ _ _ _ _ _ , says Little Bear.

_____

"

Mother Bear answers, _ _ _ _ _ _ _ _

_____

_ _ _ _ _ _ _ _ _ _ _ _ _ _ _ _ "

_____

_ _ _ _ _ _ _ _ _ _ _ _ _ _ _ .

_____

"

Little Bear says, _ _ _ _ _ _ _ _ _ _

_____

_ _ _ _ _ _ _ _ _ _ _ _ _ _ _ "

_____

_ _ _ _ _ _ _ _ _ _ _ _ _ _ _ .

" _ _ _ _ _ _ _ _ _ _ _ _ _ _ _ _ _ _

_____

_____

_ _ _ _ _ _ _ _ _ _ _ _ _ "

_____

_ _ _ _ _ _ _ _ , answers Mother Bear.

#40003—Instructional Guide: Little Bear

Name _____

Story Elements—Setting

Directions: Draw a picture of Little Bear in his bed. Make a big imagination bubble at the top of his head showing a setting of something he wished for.

Name _____

Story Elements—Plot

Directions: Reread page 53 in this story. This is the page where Little Bear wishes that he could find a Viking boat. Draw your mental image of this scene below. Then, change papers with a friend. Have your friend draw his or her mental image.

My Mental Image	_____'s Mental Image

Directions: Look closely at the pictures above. Then, finish these sentences.

1. Our mental images are the same because

_____

_____.

2. Our mental images are different because

_____

_____.

Name _____

Story Elements—Character

Directions: Draw something that Little Bear wishes for in each box. Label each of your pictures.

_____

- - - - - - - - - - - - - - - - - -

_____

- - - - - - - - - - - - - - - - - -

_____

Name _____

Post-Reading Theme Thoughts

Directions: Pretend you are Little Bear. Draw a picture of a happy face or a sad face for each statement. Then, use words to explain how he feels.

Statement	How Do You Feel? ☺ ☹	Explain How Little Bear Feels
You look and look. But, you already have what you need.		
Somebody forgot your birthday.		
You can go anywhere in your imagination.		
Time for bed!		

Culminating Activity: Stick Puppets and Reader's Theater

Directions: Reproduce the stick puppet patterns on pages 60–61 on tagboard or construction paper. Have students cut them along the dashed lines. To complete the stick puppets, glue each pattern to a tongue depressor or craft stick.

Consider the following suggestions for using the stick puppets:

- Prepare the stick puppets to use with the reader's theater script on pages 62–64. Let small groups of students take turns reading the parts and using the stick puppets.

- Let students experiment with the stick puppets by retelling the different Little Bear stories in their own words.

- Have students create new Little Bear adventures, using the stick puppets.

- If other characters are needed, have students make their own stick puppets.

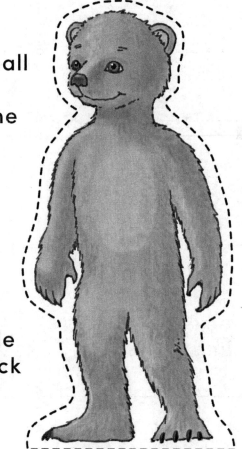

Little Bear

culminating Activity: Stick Puppets and Reader's Theater *(cont.)*

Mother Bear

Cat

culminating Activity: Stick Puppets and Reader's Theater *(cont.)*

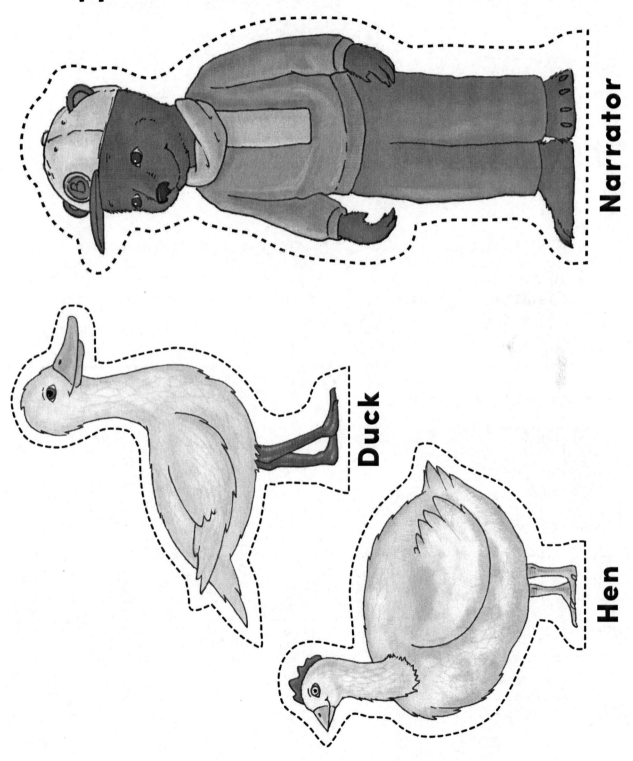

Narrator

Duck

Hen

Culminating Activity: Stick Puppets and Reader's Theater *(cont.)*

Two of Us

Characters

Narrator	**Duck**
Little Bear	**Cat**
Mother Bear	**Hen**

Narrator: Little Bear is sitting in his house when the phone rings.

Little Bear: I will get it, Mother Bear. Hello.

Duck: Hi, Little Bear.

Little Bear: Hello, Duck.

Duck: Little Bear, come quick! There is another me in my house!

Little Bear: That sounds quite surprising! I'll be right over!

Narrator: Little Bear runs over to Duck's house.

Two of Us (cont.)

Duck: Look! There's the other me!

Little Bear: Oh no! There's another one of me, too!

Narrator: Just then, Cat walks by Duck's house. Little Bear peeks out the window.

Little Bear: Hello, Cat.

Cat: Why, hello, Little Bear.

Little Bear: Come inside. We need to figure out why there is another one of Duck.

Cat: Sure, I would be glad to help. Oh my, there is another one of me as well.

Narrator: Just then, Hen walks by Duck's house.

Little Bear: Hello, Hen.

Hen: Hi, Little Bear. How are you?

Little Bear: Come inside quickly and help us figure out why there are two of each of us!

Hen: Oh my goodness! There is another of me and Cat and Duck and you!

Two of Us *(cont.)*

Narrator:	Suddenly, there is a knock at the door. Duck answers the door.
Mother Bear:	Hello, Duck. I am looking for Little Bear.
Duck:	Oh Mother Bear, please help us figure out why there are two of each of us.
Narrator:	Mother Bear comes inside Duck's house.
Mother Bear:	*(giggles)* Oh, children, you are looking at your reflections in the mirror!
Narrator:	Everyone at Duck's house laughs.
Mother Bear:	Little Bear, why don't you and your friends come back home and have lemonade and cookies.
Little Bear:	Yay!
Duck:	Hurray!
Cat:	Okay!
Hen:	Let's go!

comprehension Assessment

Directions: Fill in the bubble for the best response to each question.

"What Will Little Bear Wear?"

1. Why does Little Bear **not** need a fur coat?

   (A) He is too hot.

   (B) He is too cold.

   (C) He already has a fur coat.

   (D) He wants to come inside.

"Birthday Soup"

2. Why is Little Bear happy to see Mother Bear?

   (A) He misses her.

   (B) He is happy she did not forget his birthday.

   (C) He is scared.

   (D) He is happy she came back.

"Little Bear Goes to the Moon"

3. How does Little Bear think he will get to the moon?

   (A) He will fly.

   (B) He will go in a spaceship.

   (C) He will climb.

   (D) "'My, my,' he said. 'Here I am on the moon.'"

Name _____

comprehension Assessment (cont.)

"Little Bear's Wish"

4. What tells why Little Bear is not asleep?

(A) He is scared.

(B) "'Oh, yes, that was fun,' said Little Bear."

(C) He misses Mother Bear.

(D) "'I'm wishing,' said Little Bear."

5. Retell the story that Mother Bear tells Little Bear.

_____

- - - - - - - - - - - - - - - -

_____

_____

- - - - - - - - - - - - - - - -

_____

_____

- - - - - - - - - - - - - - - -

_____

_____

- - - - - - - - - - - - - - - -

_____

_____

Response to Literature:
The Adventures of Little Bear

Directions: Choose one scene from any of the Little Bear stories you've read. Think about which scene is your favorite. Draw a picture of that scene. Then, answer the questions on the next page about your scene. Make sure your picture is neat and is in color.

Name _____

Response to Literature:
The Adventures of Little Bear *(cont.)*

1. What is happening in the scene?

_____

- - - - - - - - - - - - - - - - - -

_____
_____

- - - - - - - - - - - - - - - - - -

_____

2. Why did you choose this scene?

_____

- - - - - - - - - - - - - - - - - -

_____
_____

- - - - - - - - - - - - - - - - - -

_____

3. What happens next in the story?

_____

- - - - - - - - - - - - - - - - - -

_____
_____

- - - - - - - - - - - - - - - - - -

_____

Response to Literature Rubric

Directions: Use this rubric to evaluate student responses to The Adventures of Little Bear activity.

Great Job	Good Work	Keep Trying
☐ You answered all three questions completely. You included many details.	☐ You answered all three questions.	☐ You did not answer all three questions.
☐ Your handwriting is very neat. There are no spelling errors.	☐ Your handwriting can be neater. There are some spelling errors.	☐ Your handwriting is not very neat. There are many spelling errors.
☐ Your picture is neat and fully colored.	☐ Your picture is neat and some of it is colored.	☐ Your picture is not very neat and/or fully colored.
☐ Creativity is clear in both the picture and the writing.	☐ Creativity is clear in either the picture or the writing.	☐ There is not much creativity in either the picture or the writing.

Teacher Comments: _____

_____

_____

_____

Writing Paper

Name _____

_____

_ _ _ _ _ _ _ _ _ _ _ _ _ _ _ _ _ _ _

_____

_____

_ _ _ _ _ _ _ _ _ _ _ _ _ _ _ _ _ _ _

_____

_ _ _ _ _ _ _ _ _ _ _ _ _ _ _ _ _ _ _

_____

_ _ _ _ _ _ _ _ _ _ _ _ _ _ _ _ _ _ _